Published by Creative Education
P.O. Box 227, Mankato, Minnesota 56002
Creative Education is an imprint of The Creative Company

Design and production by Blue Design
Printed in the United States of America

Photographs by Getty Images (Brian Bahr, Al Bello/ALLSPORT, Jeff Carlick/Allsport, ROY DABNER/AFP, Jonathan Daniel/ALLSPORT, Stephen Dunn, MIKE FIALA/AFP, Stephen Green/MLB Photos, Jeff Gross/ ALLSPORT, JEFF HAYNES/AFP, Harry How/ALLSPORT, Jed Jacobsohn/Allsport, Paul Jasienski, Vincent Laforet/Allsport, Rob Leiter/MLB Photos, JOHN G. MABANGLO/AFP, Alex Maclean, DAVID MAXWELL/AFP, Donald Miralle, Tom Pidgeon, Ezra Shaw, Don Smith/MLB Photos)

Library of Congress Cataloging-in-Publication Data

Gilbert, Sara.
The story of the Arizona Diamondbacks / by Sara Gilbert.
p. cm. — (Baseball: the great American game)
Includes index.
ISBN-13: 978-1-58341-478-1
1. Arizona Diamondbacks (Baseball team)—History—Juvenile literature. I. Title. II. Series.

GV875.A64G55 2007
796.357'640979173—dc22   2006027457

First Edition
9 8 7 6 5 4 3 2 1

Cover: Pitcher Randy Johnson
Page 1: Pitcher Curt Schilling
Page 3: Pitcher Brandon Webb

THE STORY OF THE
ARIZONA
DIAMONDBACKS

by Sara Gilbert

Arizona Diamondbacks

All they needed was a base hit. With the score tied 2–2 and the bases loaded in the bottom of the ninth inning, the Arizona Diamondbacks were one single away from winning the 2001 World Series. But with New York Yankees closer Mariano Rivera on the mound, Luis Gonzalez wasn't counting on any miracles. "Gonzo," as Arizona's goateed outfielder was known, was looking for just one good pitch to swing at. And when he saw that pitch come across the plate, he tightened his grip on the bat, stepped toward the mound, and swung. The ball sailed over shortstop Derek Jeter's head and fell in shallow center, just far enough to score second baseman Jay Bell from third. As the crowd at Bank One Ballpark erupted, the Diamondbacks gathered in a group hug around home plate. In only its fourth year of existence, Arizona had reached the pinnacle of the baseball world.

DRY IN THE DESERT

Phoenix, Arizona, is a desert city. Grand saguaro cacti, their arms reaching for the brilliant blue sky, take the place of trees, and rocks and sand substitute for grass in many yards. Citrus fruits flourish in the hot, dry air, while people seek relief in climate-controlled buildings and cars. But it's never too hot for baseball in Arizona's capital city. For decades, several major-league teams have held their spring training camps in and around Phoenix. And in 1998, the city became the home of the state's own professional team, the Arizona Diamondbacks, named after the region's native rattlesnakes.

From the day Arizona was awarded a major-league franchise in 1995, team owner Jerry Colangelo made it clear that the Diamondbacks would be a competitive team. As the roster-building process began, Colangelo raised eyebrows around the league by offering high salaries to such veterans as second baseman Jay Bell and third baseman Matt Williams and by signing young first baseman Travis Lee for $10 million. The roster wasn't the only thing Colangelo splurged on. To accommodate Diamondbacks fans on the 115-degree summer days that can occur in Phoenix, Colangelo helped finance the building of the "BOB," the $354-million Bank One Ballpark (later renamed

PHOENIX

PHOENIX – Home to almost one and a half million people, Phoenix is a widely spread city, covering about 475 square miles. The thermometer climbs above 100 degrees most summer days in this desert metropolis, making it America's hottest city.

BUCK SHOWALTER

THE DIAMONDBACKS' DEBUT

The Arizona Diamondbacks had been in the making for the better part of three years before the team finally took the field on March 31, 1998. Although they lost that first game, and the next four as well, the team played valiantly in its first major-league season. The Diamondbacks made headlines in May when manager Buck Showalter, clinging to an 8–6 lead, decided to intentionally walk fearsome San Francisco Giants slugger Barry Bonds with the bases loaded in the bottom of the ninth inning, even though it meant cutting the lead to one by sending a run home. Showalter's move paid off, as the next batter lined out to right field to end the game. Such savvy play helped the team look less like an expansion club and more like a rising contender. In September, Arizona recorded wins in 12 of the 24 games it played, including 7 in a row, tying a major-league expansion team record. Although the Diamondbacks finished the season in last place in the National League (NL) Western Division at 65–97, the groundwork for a winning team had been laid.

Chase Field). It had a retractable roof, air conditioning, and water cannons that blasted streams of water to celebrate home runs.

Those cannons sprang into action at the team's first home game, when the Diamondbacks took on the Colorado Rockies on March 31, 1998. More than 50,000 fans showed up for the opening game, hoping to see manager Buck Showalter and his fledgling Diamondbacks start the season with a bang. Lee delivered, sparking the first blast from the water cannons. The young first baseman hit the team's first single in the first inning and added another in the fourth before driving a home run into the right-field seats in the sixth,

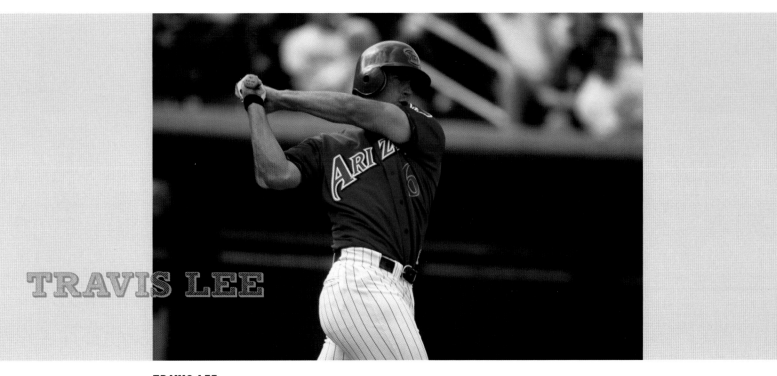

TRAVIS LEE – Lee was the second overall pick in baseball's 1996 draft but refused to play for the team that selected him, the Minnesota Twins. He spent two and a half seasons in Arizona, making noise in the franchise's first season by slugging 22 home runs.

Pro baseball was an instant hit in Arizona, as 3.6 million fans packed the new BOB over the course of the 1998 season.

scoring the first Diamondbacks run in history. But his 3-for-4 night wasn't enough; the game ended 9–2 in favor of the Rockies.

Four more losses would follow before the Diamondbacks got their first win on April 5—a 3–2 victory for pitcher Andy Benes at the BOB. Although Benes, a veteran right-hander with a hard fastball, led the pitching staff with 14 wins, Arizona struggled the rest of that first season. The team finished 65–97, landing in fifth place in the NL West. "It's disappointing," pitcher Brian Anderson said midway through the season. "I'm not going to lie. I expected this group to do a lot more."

Even as the losses added up, Arizona fans found plenty of reasons to go to the ballpark and watch their new hometown team, from witnessing their 159 home runs to enjoying the swimming pool beyond the park's center-field wall. The Diamondbacks played in front of 21 sold-out crowds and drew a total of 3,602,856 fans during the 1998 season. To thank them for their support, team owners made a concerted effort to improve the Diamondbacks' fortunes by bringing in more talent in the off-season.

PITCHER · RANDY JOHNSON

With his wild hair, shaggy moustache, and towering height, Randy Johnson was intimidating even before he started pitching. But when "The Big Unit" unleashed his 100-mile-per-hour fastball, he could flat-out terrorize opposing batters. That's exactly what he did during his first six years with the Diamondbacks. On May 8, 2001, Johnson fanned 20 batters and led the majors in strikeouts that year with 372. During each of his first four seasons with Arizona, his numerous accomplishments on the mound were honored with the NL Cy Young Award. He returned to Arizona before the 2007 season.

RANDY JOHNSON
PITCHER

ARIZONA
DIAMONDBACKS

STATS

Diamondbacks seasons: 1999–2004, 2007–present

Height: 6-10

Weight: 225

- **5-time Cy Young Award winner**
- **10-time All-Star**
- **Pitched a perfect game (May 18, 2004)**
- **4,544 career strikeouts**

TONY WOMACK

Speedster Tony Womack hit his base-stealing peak during the 1999 season, swiping an NL-high 72 bases.

TURNING UP THE HEAT

iamondbacks owner Jerry Colangelo and general manager Joe Garagiola were soon luring talented free agents to Arizona. By the time spring training started in February 1999, they had inked deals with several top-notch players—most notably veteran pitchers Randy Johnson and Todd Stottle-myre and center fielder Steve Finley, who was already a multiple Gold Glove winner. They had also orchestrated trades that brought in steady-hitting left fielder Luis Gonzalez and speedy shortstop Tony Womack.

These additions aged Arizona's roster considerably, but they also brought much-needed poise and experience to the team. Even returning veterans such as Jay Bell and Matt Williams played better in their company. Bell led the team with 38 home runs in 1999, closely followed by Williams's 35. Finley, never before known as a power hitter, added 34 of his own, and Gonzalez impressed his new fans with a break-out season: a .336 average, 26 home runs, and a league-leading 206 hits. "We were hoping for maybe .270 to .280, 15 homers, and 70 RBI," Colangelo said of Gonzalez. "Needless to say, we're pretty happy with the way things have worked out."

As potent as the offense was, however, it was the pitching staff that had

CATCHER · DAMIAN MILLER

It takes a special kind of catcher to handle the blistering fastballs hurled by Randy Johnson. But Damian Miller was up to the task. Miller, who played his first major-league season with the Minnesota Twins in 1997 before going to Arizona in the 1998 expansion draft, became known as Johnson's personal backstop because of the skillful manner in which he handled the 6-foot-10, flamethrowing pitcher. But apart from his excellent glove work, Miller could also hold his own at the plate. He maintained a .270 or better average in four of his five years in a Diamondbacks uniform.

STATS

Diamondbacks seasons: 1998–2002

Height: 6-3

Weight: 202

- **2002 All-Star**
- **382 career RBI**
- **.264 career BA**
- **196 career doubles**

DAMIAN MILLER
CATCHER

ARIZONA
DIAMONDBACKS

MATT WILLIAMS

MATT WILLIAMS – Williams earned a prominent place in the Diamondbacks' record books by driving in a club-record 142 runs in 1999. A dependable fielder and clutch hitter, he played in World Series with three teams (Giants, Indians, and Diamondbacks).

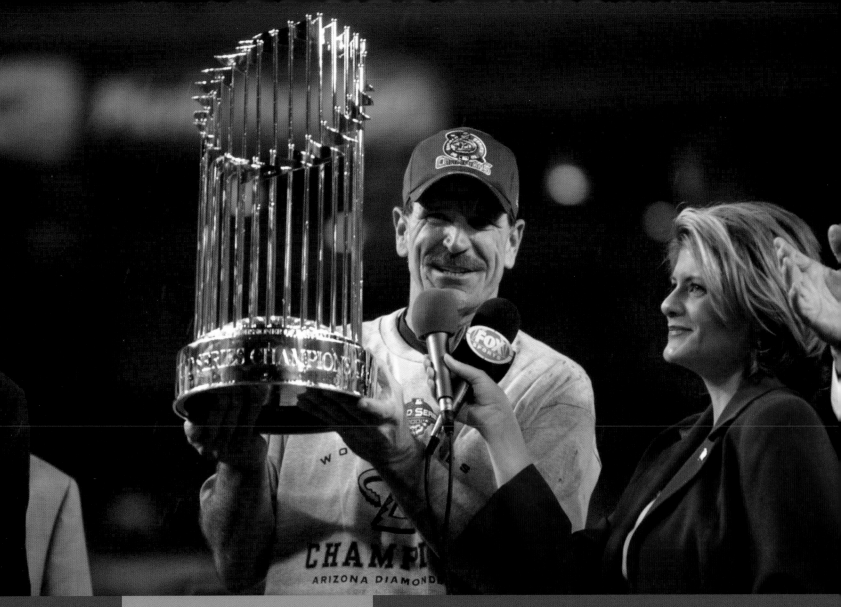

FOUR-YEAR FORMULA

After failing to lead Arizona to the top in its first three seasons, manager Buck Showalter was replaced in 2001 by Bob Brenly, who had no experience as a major-league skipper. If that seems a bit unorthodox, consider the team he was managing. Not a single regular player had been developed in Arizona's farm system. Instead, the four-year-old team was populated by seasoned veterans, such as second baseman Jay Bell and third baseman Matt Williams, who had been lured away from other teams with large salaries and the promise of playing for a competitive team. It soon became apparent that they were: By the time the Diamondbacks claimed

first place in May, it was clear that they intended to be contenders. Arizona clinched the NL West crown for the second time, and by the end of October, the Diamondbacks were on their way to the World Series after defeating the St. Louis Cardinals in the NL Division Series (NLDS) and overtaking the Atlanta Braves in the NL Championship Series (NLCS). And as November got underway, the Diamondbacks were celebrating their seven-game victory over the Yankees. "We did everything we could to get the job done," said team owner Jerry Colangelo. "The opportunity was there, so we went for it."

improved the most. Benes contributed 13 wins, and Omar Daal doubled his totals in the win column to 16, but it was Johnson who had the biggest impact. "The Big Unit" tallied 17 wins, led the majors with 364 strikeouts, and led the league with a 2.48 earned run average (ERA)—numbers that earned him the NL Cy Young Award as the league's best pitcher.

With so many players enjoying career-best seasons, the Diamondbacks were able to secure the division lead early on. Gonzalez put together a 30-game hitting streak that lasted from April 11 until May 20, helping the team finish May with 18 wins and in first place in the NL West. At season's end, the Diamondbacks were 100–62 and had achieved the fastest ascent (two seasons) to a division championship in major-league history.

In the playoffs, Arizona met the New York Mets in a best-of-five NLDS. The Mets took the first game at the BOB, but Stottlemyre held New York to just four hits and one run in the second game, leveling the series as the teams headed to "The Big Apple" for Games 3 and 4. But the Diamondbacks' luck had run out. The Mets won the next two games, including one in which an extra-inning home run slipped out of Finley's usually flawless glove. A disappointed Showalter tried to reassure his players that better days were ahead. "I told them the pain will pass," he said to reporters.

FIRST BASEMAN · MARK GRACE

Mark Grace joined the Diamondbacks at just the right time. After 13 years with the Chicago Cubs, the joke-cracking, Gold Glove-winning, steady-hitting first baseman needed a change of scenery and signed with Arizona following the 2000 season. In his first year with the team, "Amazing Grace" hit .298 with 78 RBI and helped the Diamondbacks win a world championship—the first of his career. Grace, always respected for his consistency rather than his flashiness, ended his 16-year career after the 2003 season with a lifetime on-base percentage of .383, almost 2,500 hits, and more than 500 doubles.

MARK GRACE
FIRST BASEMAN

ARIZONA
DIAMONDBACKS

STATS

Diamondbacks seasons: 2001–03

Height: 6-2

Weight: 190

- **3-time All-Star**

- **4-time Gold Glove winner**

- **.303 career BA**

- **2,445 career hits**

Before joining Arizona, Andy Benes became the all-time strikeout leader in the San Diego Padres' history.

ANDY BENES

BOB BRENLY

BOB BRENLY – Before taking over as Arizona's manager in 2001, Brenly spent eight seasons playing in the majors (making one All-Star Game in 1984), four years coaching, and seven years covering the game as a radio and then television broadcaster.

But better days didn't come in 2000. Although the roster remained almost unchanged, the Diamondbacks couldn't repeat the previous season's success. The team was slowed by injuries to Williams, Stottlemyre, and closer Matt Mantei, each of whom was sidelined for a portion of the season. And although Johnson, who put together another Cy Young Award-winning season, got some help when the team acquired star pitcher Curt Schilling in July, Arizona finished third in the NL West. Showalter was fired soon after, and Colangelo started looking for a new leader.

LEADERS OF THE PACK

ew Arizona manager Bob Brenly, a former big-league catcher, coach, and broadcaster, opened his spring training meeting in 2001 by abandoning all the rules Showalter had previously laid down. "I only have two rules," he told the players. Then he showed them a cocktail napkin on which he had scrawled, "Be on time" and "Get it done."

Brenly's approach seemed to be just the change Arizona needed. Veteran players, including two off-season acquisitions—first baseman Mark Grace and right fielder Reggie Sanders—responded especially well to his more relaxed structure. Gonzalez enjoyed a monster season, sending 57 balls into the stands and driving 142 runs home. Johnson and Schilling combined for 43 wins, accounting for almost half of the team's total victories, and closer Byung-Hyun Kim notched 19 saves. The Diamondbacks climbed to a four-game division lead by the end of August, and during the final week of the season, they clinched their second division championship.

With the pain of their first postseason loss still fresh in their minds, the Diamondbacks charged into the NLDS against the St. Louis Cardinals, winning the first game 1–0, courtesy of a three-hit, complete-game effort by Schilling. The Cardinals came back to win 4–1 in Game 2, but second baseman Craig Counsell ensured a Game 3 win for the Diamondbacks with a three-run homer that put Arizona ahead 5–3. When St. Louis won Game 4 to force a deciding fifth game, the Diamondbacks returned to the BOB and wrapped up the series, winning 2–1. "We gave the fans everything they could want in this series," said Schilling, who pitched all nine innings of Game 5.

If Schilling was the star of the NLDS, Johnson was the hero of the 2001 NLCS against the Atlanta Braves. He pitched a three-hit complete game against Atlanta ace Greg Maddux in Game 1, setting the stage for a four-games-to-one series victory that sent the Diamondbacks to the World Series

DIAMONDBACKS

SECOND BASEMAN · CRAIG COUNSELL

Although it had been only three years since he scored the winning run of the 1997 World Series for the Florida Marlins, Craig Counsell was in a slump when he joined the Diamondbacks in 2000. To get out of it, he developed an unusual batting stance: he stood with his 6-foot frame barely bent, lifted his arms shoulder high, pointed his bat straight up, and then wagged it back and forth. Because of that stance, "the Pancake" (his well-worn, floppy glove), and his stints with five different teams, Counsell became one of the most recognizable players in baseball.

CRAIG COUNSELL
SECOND BASEMAN

ARIZONA
DIAMONDBACKS

STATS

Diamondbacks seasons: 2000–03, 2005–06

Height: 6-0

Weight: 184

• .985 career fielding percentage

• 2001 NLCS MVP

• .260 career BA

• 283 career RBI

to face the heavily favored New York Yankees.

The first two games were played in Phoenix, where Schilling and Johnson combined for a one-two knockout of the Yankees. In Game 1, Schilling yielded only three hits in seven innings, and Gonzalez powered the Diamondbacks to a 9–1 win with his two-run homer. The next night, Johnson struck out 11 batters in a decisive 4–0 victory. With a two-game lead, Arizona went east to play in the venerable but raucous Yankee Stadium. For many Diamond-backs players, it was their first encounter with the vocal and fiercely loyal New York fans. "We know they're not going to open their arms and welcome us in a friendly way," Gonzalez said. "I think there will be no bigger thrill than walking out to Yankee Stadium and knowing that the crowd hates us."

The city of New York, along with the rest of the country, was still reeling from the terror attacks of September 11, 2001, when the Diamondbacks arrived in town. The team paid its respects at Ground Zero before the series started and then saw President George W. Bush throw out the ceremonial first pitch before Game 3, which Arizona lost 2–1. But the

CURT SCHILLING

Diamondbacks got down to business in Game 4. Schilling, pitching on just three days' rest, had given up only one run when he left the game in the seventh inning. Then Byung-Hyun Kim gave up a two-run home run that sent the game into a 10th inning, and Yankees shortstop Derek Jeter ended the game with a long shot into the right-field stands. A tied Game 5 went into the 12th inning before the Yanks pulled out a 3–2 win. With New York up three games to two, the teams headed back to Arizona.

Game 6 was all about Arizona. The Diamondbacks scored 15 runs on 22 hits, including three from right fielder Danny Bautista, while Johnson held

LUIS GONZALEZ – "Gonzo" played nine big-league seasons—with three different teams—before hitting his stride in Arizona. From 1999 to 2006, he averaged 28 homers a season, and in the 2001 World Series, he got the single biggest hit in club history.

THIRD BASEMAN · MATT WILLIAMS

In 1986, the San Francisco Giants selected Matt Williams with the third overall pick of the amateur draft. Twelve years later, when he joined the Diamondbacks in 1998, he was known for his ability to drive home runs to all parts of the field. But long balls weren't his only specialty; Williams was also a slick fielder who manned the "hot corner" of the infield so well that he earned four Gold Gloves. Although injuries and an arthritis-like condition slowed his production toward the end of his career, he was nonetheless an important part of Arizona's 2001 world championship team.

STATS

Diamondbacks seasons: 1998–2003

Height: 6-2

Weight: 210

- 5-time All-Star

- 4-time Gold Glove winner

- 378 career HR

- 1,218 career RBI

MATT WILLIAMS
THIRD BASEMAN

ARIZONA
DIAMONDBACKS

the Yankees to just two runs. Game 7 featured Schilling in a battle against Roger Clemens. The future Hall-of-Famers kept the game scoreless until the sixth inning, when Bautista doubled in a run. After the Yanks scored twice, Schilling was sent to the bench and Miguel Batista took the mound. Batista got just one man out before an unexpected reliever was called in: Randy Johnson, who was less than 24 hours removed from his last pitching performance. Johnson faced four batters and retired them all. But in the bottom of the ninth, New York still had a 2–1 lead, and its ace closer, the intimidating Mariano Rivera, was on the mound.

Arizona's Mark Grace led the inning off with a single. Then, catcher Damian Miller reached first on a fielder's choice. One out later, Womack doubled in a run to tie the game, and Counsell was hit by a pitch, loading the bases. All that Arizona needed when Gonzalez stepped to the plate was a base hit. And "Gonzo" obliged, sending a bloop single into shallow center to score the winning run. Only four years into their existence, the Arizona Diamondbacks had won a world championship—which didn't surprise them one bit. "From day one, our goal wasn't just to get to the World Series," Gonzalez said after the game. "It was to win it." Shortly after the series ended, the team held a parade in Phoenix's Copper Square, and more than 300,000 exuberant fans turned out to congratulate their summertime heroes.

Phoenix celebrated the Diamondbacks' 2001 championship with a victory parade through the city's streets.

SHORTSTOP · TONY WOMACK

Tony Womack was every catcher's nightmare. Arizona's compact, fleet-footed shortstop made stealing bases an art form. He had to learn to play in the outfield when he first joined the team in 1999, since the middle infield was already well staffed. But his productivity on the bases was more important to the team than anything else. In his first season with the Diamondbacks, he led the league with a career-high 72 stolen bases. That same season, he hit an inside-the-park grand slam that turned a 4–3 Arizona deficit into an unlikely 7–4 victory against the Houston Astros.

TONY WOMACK
SHORTSTOP

ARIZONA DIAMONDBACKS

STATS

Diamondbacks seasons: 1999–2002

Height: 5-9

Weight: 160

- **3-time NL leader in steals**

- **363 career stolen bases**

- **.273 career BA**

- **24-game hitting streak in 2001**

LEFT FIELDER · LUIS GONZALEZ

Before being traded to the Diamondbacks in 1999, Luis Gonzalez was a solid contact hitter better known for line drives than home runs. But when "Gonzo" came to Arizona, the skinny outfielder turned into a home-run-hitting slugger. In 2001, he helped catapult the Diamondbacks to the World Series with 57 home runs, 142 RBI, and a .325 batting average. Despite that power, it took only a bloop single off of Gonzalez's bat to drive in the dramatic, series-clinching run in Game 7, making the Diamondbacks world champions in only their fourth year of existence.

LUIS GONZALEZ
LEFT FIELDER

ARIZONA
DIAMONDBACKS

STATS

Diamondbacks seasons: 1999–2006

Height: 6-2

Weight: 200

- **5-time All-Star**

- **30-game hitting streak in 1999**

- **2,373 career hits**

- **1,324 career RBI**

TRANSITION TIME

Those fans, and Arizona's players, were expecting the same sort of success the following season. Most of the team's key players returned, and management had bolstered the pitching staff by bringing in right-handed starter Rick Helling and relief specialist Mike Myers during the off-season. But before spring training was through, injuries had taken a toll on the 2002 Diamondbacks: Williams and Bell went down with leg injuries, and reserve first baseman Erubiel Durazo broke his wrist. In May, Bautista suffered a season-ending shoulder injury as well.

Even with their beleaguered lineup, the Diamondbacks took possession of first place in the division in May and hovered there throughout July, thanks to the fine pitching of Johnson and Schilling. Arizona took control of the NL West again in August by winning 19 games. But before the Diamondbacks could clinch another title, more injuries struck. Counsell missed the last two months of the season with a pinched nerve that needed surgery, and Gonzalez separated his shoulder while making a sliding catch. It took until the second-to-last game of the season for the banged-up Diamondbacks to wrap up the division crown.

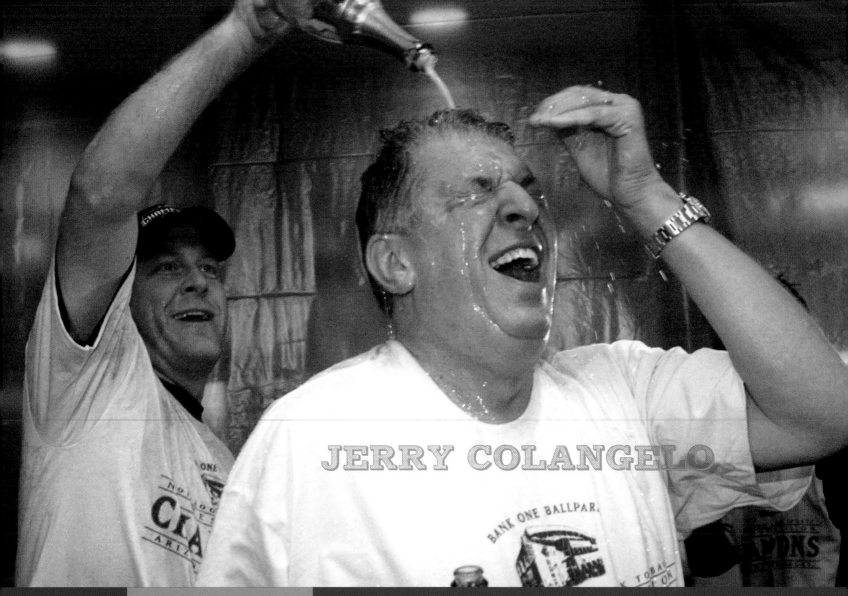

JERRY COLANGELO

DEEP POCKETS

It took more than raw talent to turn the Diamondbacks into world champions in just four years. It also took a tremendous financial commitment from the team's owner, who paid dearly to produce a winning team in Arizona. Although many owners were appalled at the salaries Jerry Colangelo was willing to offer, he was determined to pay for perfection. Before the team's debut in 1998, he paid former Kansas City Royals shortstop Jay Bell $34 million for five years and Cleveland Indians third baseman Matt Williams $49.5 million for six years—deals that Colangelo said had as much to do with their character as with their playing ability. He dug even deeper in 1999, when he negotiated a four-year, $52-million contract with star pitcher Randy Johnson, making him the second-highest paid player in baseball at the time, and offered outfielder Steve Finley a five-year, $25.5-million contract. By the time the 1999 season started, the team's payroll was at $65.9 million—more than twice what it had been in 1998. Although continuing drop-offs in season ticket sales left the team hurting for money, Colangelo's plan worked. The Diamondbacks won the NL West that year, and by 2001, on an $81-million budget, they became world champions.

CENTER FIELDER · STEVE FINLEY

Steve Finley was no stranger to grass stains. His speed and instincts helped him successfully track down and dive for balls that would have fallen in front of most other outfielders. Although such acrobatic fielding earned him five Gold Glove awards, it also caused him great pain. Finley suffered many nagging injuries but managed to play through most of them; in 1999, he hit two home runs in one game while suffering from a bulging disc in his back. The consistent line-drive hitter polished his home run stroke in Arizona: he homered 34 times in 1999 and 35 times in 2000.

STEVE FINLEY
CENTER FIELDER

ARIZONA
DIAMONDBACKS

STATS

Diamondbacks seasons: 1999–2004

Height: 6-2

Weight: 180

- **2-time All-Star**

- **5-time Gold Glove winner**

- **.988 career fielding percentage**

- **303 career HR**

By then, the team was so badly battered that it was no match for the Cardinals in the NLDS. St. Louis made quick work of the Diamondbacks, sweeping the series in three games and putting an end to Arizona's hopes of a repeat. All of the injuries had added up for Arizona. "It puts a strain on the offense," Brenly said after the series ended. "It gives the opposition the opportunity to pitch around the hitters they think can hurt them the most. It started to show up at the end of the season, and really here in the playoffs."

Things would get worse before they got better. The 2003 season had barely started when Randy Johnson was placed on the disabled list (DL) with an inflamed right knee. Schilling soon followed suit, first for an emergency appendectomy and then again a month later with a broken bone in his pitching hand. To make matters worse, a total of four position players, including Counsell, spent time on the DL in June.

Suddenly, the formerly veteran-heavy team was populated with youngsters pulled from the minor leagues to fill out the roster. Thirteen rookies debuted over the course of the 2003 season, including pitcher Brandon Webb, who did his best to fill the shoes of the absent starters by winning 10 games and posting a 2.84 ERA. Despite his valiant efforts and the midseason acquisitions of first baseman Shea Hillenbrand and left fielder Raul Mondesi,

MIKE MYERS

MIKE MYERS – Known for his submarine (or almost underhand) delivery, Myers was one of the game's steadiest relievers. His odd throwing style and curving pitches made him an effective pitcher against star left-handed sluggers such as Barry Bonds.

RIGHT FIELDER · DANNY BAUTISTA

Danny Bautista had been bouncing around the major leagues for the better part of a decade when, in June 2000, he was traded to Arizona. A little stability did him good. He had the best offensive years of his career in Arizona, hitting above .300 in 2000, 2001, and 2002. When the longtime reserve earned a starting spot in 2004, he showed his stuff by putting together a 21-game hitting streak and ended the season with a career-high 154 hits. Unfortunately, an ankle injury the following spring ended his career. Bautista retired in March 2005 at the age of 33.

STATS

Diamondbacks seasons: 2000–04

Height: 5-11

Weight: 170

- **685 career hits**
- **319 career RBI**
- **.272 career BA**
- **.984 career fielding percentage**

DANNY BAUTISTA
RIGHT FIELDER

ARIZONA
DIAMONDBACKS

Arizona fans had high hopes for 6-foot-8 Richie Sexson, but he spent just one injury-plagued season in the desert.

Arizona couldn't climb back into contention. The team ended respectably, 84–78, but was well outside of the playoff picture.

Afterwards, Mark Grace and Matt Williams retired, and Arizona management set about revamping the roster, this time in favor of power and youth. In November, Schilling was sent to the Boston Red Sox for two younger pitchers. Days later, six more players were traded to the Milwaukee Brewers in exchange for slugging first baseman Richie Sexson. "It's going to be exciting to watch him," Arizona general manager Joe Garagiola said of Sexson. "This will give our whole lineup a very different look."

THE PERFECT GAME

Randy Johnson was 40 years old when he took the mound at Atlanta's Turner Field on the night of May 18, 2004. After four consecutive Cy Young Award-winning seasons with the Arizona Diamondbacks, Johnson had suffered through a miserable, injury-plagued season in 2003 and had been subject to criticism over his 3–4 start in 2004. But on that spring night against the Atlanta Braves, Johnson silenced his critics the best way possible: by eliminating all 27 batters he faced and throwing the 17th perfect game in major-league history—the first no-hitter of any sort for the Arizona franchise. Johnson struck out 13 batters and threw 18 pitches that were clocked at 97 miles per hour or faster—including a 98-mile-per-hour fastball that pinch hitter Eddie Perez swung through for the last out of the game. Johnson ended the game having tossed a total of 117 pitches, more than half of them for strikes. Johnson, who had pitched a no-hitter 14 years earlier as an up-and-coming member of the Seattle Mariners, seemed unfazed by the achievement as his teammates crowded around him with congratulations. "Not bad for being 40 years old," he said. "Everything was locked in."

RANDY JOHNSON

STARTING OVER

The 2004 Arizona lineup did indeed have a new look: Sexson started at first, Roberto Alomar at second, Chad Tracy at third, Scott Hairston at shortstop, and Luis Terrero with Gonzalez and Finley in the outfield. But the cornerstone of that new look didn't last for long. Just days after hitting the longest home run (503 feet) in the history of the BOB in April, Sexson partially dislocated his shoulder during a check swing. When he attempted to make a comeback in May, he re-aggravated the injury and had to have surgery, effectively ending his season.

Amid all the changes around the field, Randy Johnson remained the main man on the mound. Unfortunately, the rotation behind him no longer had much depth. Webb posted only 7 wins, second-best to Johnson's 16, and no other pitcher recorded even 5 wins. After enduring a 14-game midseason losing streak, the Diamondbacks finished 2004 with a dismal 51–111 mark, at the bottom of the heap in the NL West.

The team made two big moves before the 2005 season, hiring former Arizona bench coach Bob Melvin as manager, and trading Johnson to the New York Yankees. Slugging third baseman Troy Glaus and veteran outfielder

DIAMONDBACKS

Scott Hairston spent time at both infield and outfield positions in his first three big-league seasons (2004–06).

SCOTT HAIRSTON

MANAGER · BOB BRENLY

Bob Brenly, a former catcher for the San Francisco Giants, started his first season as manager of the Diamondbacks with a team full of veteran players. Although some of those players were only 10 years his junior, Brenly took firm control of the team when he was hired after the 2000 season. Under his laid-back leadership, the 2001 Diamondbacks cruised to a 92–70 record, tops in the NL West, and upset the powerful New York Yankees in the World Series. Although Brenly's team repeated as division champs in 2002, he was fired after a midseason slide in 2004.

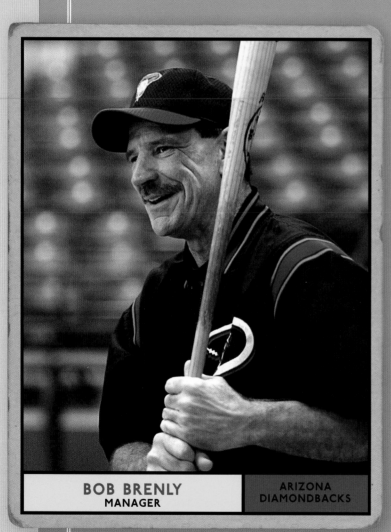

BOB BRENLY
MANAGER

ARIZONA
DIAMONDBACKS

STATS

Diamondbacks seasons as manager:
  2001–04

Height: 6-2

Weight: 210

Managerial Record: 303–262

World Series Championship: 2001

BASEBALL AT THE BOB

When Jerry Colangelo first met with baseball owners in 1993 to discuss bringing a major-league team to Arizona, he painted an idyllic picture of the park in which his team would play: a state-of-the-art stadium with a retractable roof, natural grass, and a swimming pool and jacuzzi just beyond the center-field wall. By the time ground was broken for the $354-million downtown Phoenix facility in November 1995, the plans had evolved even further. The field was designed with a dirt path between the pitcher's mound and home plate, reminiscent of early ballparks, and celebratory water cannons were added to the outfield. Almost two and a half years later, the 49,033-seat stadium opened—complete with all of Colangelo's promised features. The roof opened and closed to a specially composed soundtrack timed to last exactly the four and a half minutes required to move the steel structure. The pool and spa, which got a facelift in 2005, have hosted more than 20,000 visitors—and a few long home runs as well. The first player to send a ball splashing into the pool was Mark Grace, who homered as a member of the Chicago Cubs on May 12, 1998. The stadium was renamed Chase Field in 2005.

DIAMONDBACKS

AL PEDRIQUE

BACK TO THE BOTTOM

The 2004 Diamondbacks were a team in transition. Many of the key players who had been paid top dollar to lead the team to a world championship in 2001 had either retired, been traded, or left the team via free agency—and with ownership concerned about a lack of revenue, their salaries weren't about to be replaced. By midseason, manager Bob Brenly was also gone, fired after Arizona fell to 29–51 in early July. But things didn't get any better for interim manager Al Pedrique, who went into the All-Star break with a three-game losing streak and came out of it having lost 11 more. The roster of untested rookies and aging, injury-prone veterans struggled to put together more than two or three wins at a time. By the time September mercifully ended, the Diamondbacks were 51–111, the worst in the NL. Along the way, star pitcher Randy Johnson had picked up his 100th win with Arizona on September 10 (his 41st birthday) and earned bragging rights as major league baseball's all-time left-handed strikeout leader. But as had been rumored throughout the year, Johnson was traded away to the Yankees in the off-season, making room for younger Diamondbacks players on the 2005 roster.

Shawn Green spent the 2005 season in Arizona, but the Diamondbacks finished 77–85 and out of the playoffs again.

Webb was the star of Arizona's 2006 season, as the maturing pitcher won 16 games to earn the Cy Young Award. And even though the team finished only one victory better than it had the season before, Arizona general manager John Byrnes liked what the Diamondbacks had brewing. Randy Johnson returned to the team from New York in the off-season, and as they prepared to open 2007 in redesigned, red- and sand-colored uniforms, the Diamondbacks also prepared to unveil the future of the team. Gone were past heroes such as Gonzalez, replaced by such youngsters as sweet-swinging shortstop Stephen Drew, brawny first baseman Conor Jackson, and swift outfielder Chris Young. "These guys are ready to perform," said Byrnes. "It's becoming their team."

In less than a decade, the Diamondbacks have experienced the highest highs an expansion team could hope for—and some low points as well. Fans hope that the not-so-distant memory of the club's 2001 world title will help inspire the new-look franchise and its young players to soon bring championship-caliber baseball back to the Arizona desert.